HISTORY'S MOST INFLUENTIAL
SCIENTISTS

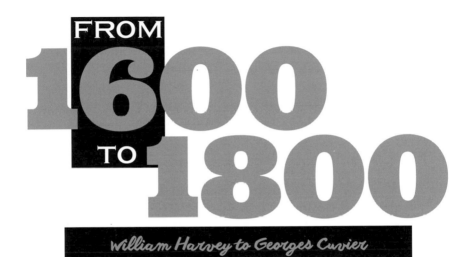

FROM

1600
TO 1800

William Harvey to Georges Cuvier

EDITED BY KATE ROGERS

Britannica®
Educational Publishing

IN ASSOCIATION WITH

ROSEN
EDUCATIONAL SERVICES

T0051187

Published in 2024 by Britannica Educational Publishing
(a trademark of Encyclopædia Britannica, Inc.)
in association with Rosen Educational Services, LLC
2544 Clinton Street, Buffalo, NY 14224.

Distributed exclusively by Rosen Educational Services.
For a listing of additional Britannica Educational Publishing titles, call toll free (800) 237-9932.

First Edition

Britannica Educational Publishing
Michael I. Levy: Executive Editor
Marilyn L. Barton: Senior Coordinator, Production Control
Steven Bosco: Director, Editorial Technologies
Lisa S. Braucher: Senior Producer and Data Editor
Yvette Charboneau: Senior Copy Editor
Kathy Nakamura: Manager, Media Acquisition
Kara Rogers: Senior Editor, Biomedical Sciences

Editor: Greg Roza
Book design: Michael Flynn

Photo credits: Cover https://commons.wikimedia.org/wiki/File:Portrait_of_Sir_Isaac_
Newton,_1689.jpg; p. 9 https://commons.wikimedia.org/wiki/File:William_Harvey_
(1578-1657)_Venenbild.jpg; p. 22 Everett Collection/Shutterstock.com.

Cataloging-in-Publication Data

Names: Rogers, Kate.
Title: Influential scientists: from 1600 to 1800 —William Harvey to Georges Cuvier / Kate
Rogers.
Description: New York : Britannica Educational Publishing, in Association with Rosen
Educational Services. 2024. | Series: History's most influential scientists | Includes
glossary and index.
Identifiers: ISBN 9781499474763 (library bound) | ISBN 9781499474756 (pbk) | ISBN
9781499474770 (ebook)
Subjects: LCSH: Scientists--Biography--Juvenile literature. | Science--History--Juvenile
literature. | Discoveries in science--Juvenile literature.

Classification: LCC Q141.R64 2024 | DDC 509.2'2 B--dc23

CONTENTS

INTRODUCTION

Very many maintain that all we know is still infinitely less than all that still remains unknown.
—William Harvey (1578–1657)

From the very first moment humans appeared on the planet, we have attempted to understand and explain the world around us. The most insatiably curious among us often have become scientists.

The scientists discussed in this book have shaped humankind's knowledge and laid the foundation for virtually every scientific discipline. Some of these individuals pondered questions about what was contained within the human body, while others were intrigued by celestial bodies. Their collective vision has been concentrated enough to examine microscopic particles and broad enough to unlock tremendous universal marvels such as gravity, relativity—even the nature of life itself.

Many early scientists studied several different branches during their lifetimes. Great thinkers of the ancient world and the Renaissance laid the foundations for later advancements in chemistry, biology, physics, zoology, botany, psychology, astronomy, and more by the scientists who followed.

In the 1600s, Englishman William Harvey paved the way for modern physiology with his numerous animal dissections. Harvey was the first person to describe the function of the circulatory system, providing evidence that veins and arteries had separate and distinct functions.

Other groundbreaking scientists relied on observations outside the body. A gifted Dutch scientist and lens grinder named Antonie van Leeuwenhoek refined the main tool of his trade, the microscope, which allowed him to become the first person to observe tiny microbes. Leeuwenhoek's observations helped build the framework for bacteriology and protozoology.

Then there are the numerous scientific advances that began with the development of vaccines. Smallpox was a leading cause of death in 18th-century England. Yet Edward Jenner, an English surgeon, noticed that people who were exposed to cowpox, a disease contracted from infected cattle that had relatively minor symptoms, did not get smallpox. Concluding that cowpox could offer protection, Jenner purposely infected a young boy who lived in the village first with cowpox, then with smallpox. Jenner successfully administered the world's first vaccine.

Medical scientists are certainly not the only ones to build on one another's work. Discoveries of one scientist are almost always examined, recreated, and expanded on by others. Luigi Galvani, an Italian physicist and physician, for example, discovered that animal tissue (specifically frog legs) could conduct an electric current. Building on Galvani's observations, his friend, Italian scientist Alessandro Volta, constructed the first battery in 1800.

In 1675, Isaac Newton wrote a letter to Robert Hooke in which he said, "If I have seen further it is by standing on the shoulders of giants." Thanks to their predecessors, today's scientists have a solid foundation upon which to make astounding leaps of logic. Without the work of these men and women, we would not have computers, electricity, or many modern conveniences. We would not have the vaccines and medications that help keep us healthy. And, in general, we would know a lot less about the way the human body functions and the way the world works. Today's scientists owe a huge debt of gratitude to the scientists of days past. By standing on the shoulders of these giants, who knows how far they may be able to see.

WILLIAM HARVEY

(b. April 1, 1578, Folkestone, Kent, Eng.—d. June 3, 1657, London)

English physician William Harvey was the first to recognize the full circulation of the blood in the human body and to provide experiments and arguments to support this idea.

DISCOVERY OF CIRCULATION

Harvey's key work was *Exercitatio Anatomica de Motu Cordis et Sanguinis in Animalibus* (*Anatomical Exercise on the Motion of the Heart and Blood in Animals*), published in 1628. Harvey's greatest achievement was to recognize that the blood flows rapidly around the human body, being pumped through a single system of arteries and veins, and to support this hypothesis with experiments and arguments.

Prior to Harvey, it was believed there were two separate blood systems in the body. One carried purple, "nutritive" blood and used the veins to distribute nutrition from the liver to the rest of the body. The other carried scarlet, "vivyfying" (or "vital") blood and used the arteries to distribute a life-giving principle from the lungs. Today these blood systems are understood as deoxygenated blood and oxygenated blood. However, at the time, the influence of oxygen on blood was not understood. Furthermore, blood was not thought to circulate around the body—it was believed to be consumed by the body at the same rate that it was produced. The capillaries, small vessels linking the arteries and veins, were unknown at the time, and their existence was not confirmed until later in the 17th century, after Harvey, when the microscope had been invented.

Harvey claimed he was led to his discovery of the

circulation by consideration of the venous valves. It was known that there were small flaps inside the veins that allowed free passage of blood in one direction but strongly inhibited the flow of blood in the opposite direction. It was thought that these flaps prevented pooling of the blood under the influence of gravity, but Harvey was able to show that all these flaps are cardiocentrically oriented. For example, he showed that in the jugular vein of the neck they face downward, inhibiting blood flow away from the heart, instead of upward, inhibiting pooling due to gravity.

Harvey's main experiment concerned the amount of blood flowing through the heart. He made estimates of the volume of the ventricles, how efficient they were in expelling blood, and the number of beats per minute made by the heart. He was able to show, even with conservative estimates, that more blood passed through the heart than could possibly be accounted for based on the then current understanding of blood flow. Harvey's values indicated the heart pumped 1.05–2.11 pints (0.5–1 L) of blood per minute (modern values are about 8.5 pints (4 L) per minute at rest and 52.8 pints (25 L) per minute during exercise). The human body contains about 10.5 pints (5 L) of blood. The body simply could not produce or consume that amount of blood so rapidly; therefore, the blood had to circulate.

It is also important that Harvey investigated the nature of the heartbeat. Prior to Harvey, it was thought that the active phase of the heartbeat, when the muscles contract, was when the heart increased its internal volume. So the active motion of the heart was to draw blood into itself. Harvey observed the heart beating in many animals—particularly in cold-blooded animals and in animals near death, because their heartbeats were slow. He concluded that the active phase of the heartbeat, when the muscles contract, is when the heart decreases its internal volume and that blood is expelled with considerable force from the heart. Although Harvey did quantify blood flow, his quantification is very approximate, and he deliberately used underestimates to further his case. This is very different from the precise quantification leading to the mathematical laws of someone like Galileo.

Harvey's theory of circulation was opposed by conservative physicians, but it was well established by the time of his death. It is likely that Harvey actually made his discovery of the circulation about 1618–19. Such a major shift in thinking about the body needed to be very well supported by experiment and argument to avoid immediate ridicule and dismissal; hence the delay before the publication of his central work. In 1649 Harvey published *Exercitationes Duae Anatomicae de Circulatione Sanguinis, ad Joannem Riolanem, Filium, Parisiensem* (*Two Anatomical Exercises on the Circulation of the Blood*) in response to criticism of the circulation theory by French anatomist Jean Riolan.

Renaissance Influences

Harvey was very much influenced by the ideas of Greek philosopher Aristotle and the natural magic tradition of the Renaissance. His key analogy for the circulation of the blood was a macrocosm/microcosm analogy with the weather system. A macrocosm/microcosm analogy sees similarities between a small system and a large system. Thus, one might say that the solar system is a macrocosm and the atom is a microcosm. The Renaissance natural magic tradition was very keen on the idea of the human body as a microcosm. The macrocosm for Harvey was Earth's weather cycle. Water was changed into vapor by the action of the sun, and the vapor rose, was cooled, and fell again as rain. The microcosm was the human body, where the action of the heart was supposed to heat and

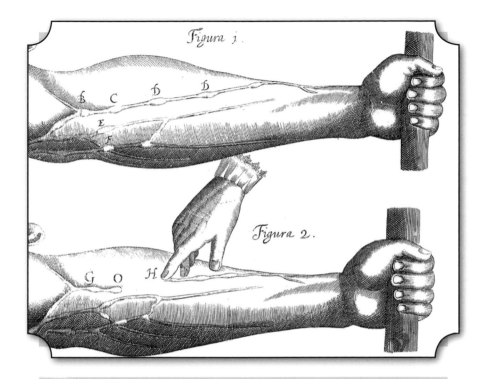

This engraving from a groundbreaking work by the physician and human anatomy expert William Harvey demonstrates how blood flows through the veins of the arm.

change the blood, which was cooled again in the extremities of the body. It also should be noted that much of his terminology for change was drawn from the alchemy of his time. Harvey was very much a man of the later Renaissance—not a man of the scientific revolution and its mechanical nature.

STUDIES OF REPRODUCTION

Harvey spent much of the latter part of his career working on the nature of reproduction in animals. He worked on chickens as an example of oviparous reproduction, in which embryonic development occurs within eggs hatched outside the mother's body, and on deer as an example of viviparous reproduction, in which embryonic development occurs within the mother's body, resulting in the birth of live young. Harvey's work in this area generated a wealth of observational detail. At the time, reproduction was poorly understood, and Harvey investigated issues of the role of sperm and menstrual blood in the formation of the embryo. His observations were excellent, but such matters could not be resolved properly without the use of the microscope.

ROBERT BOYLE

(b. Jan. 25, 1627, Lismore Castle, County Waterford, Ire.—d. Dec. 31, 1691, London, Eng.)

British natural philosopher and theological writer Robert Boyle was a preeminent figure of 17th-century intellectual culture. He was best known as a natural philosopher, particularly in the field of chemistry, but his scientific work covered many areas including hydrostatics, physics, medicine, earth sciences, natural history, and alchemy. His prolific output also included Christian devotional and ethical essays and theological tracts on biblical language, the limits of reason, and the role of the natural philosopher as a Christian. He sponsored many religious missions as well as the translation of the scriptures into several languages. In 1660 he helped found the Royal Society of London.

Boyle spent much of 1652–54 in Ireland overseeing his hereditary lands, and he also performed some anatomic dissections. In 1654 he was invited to Oxford, and he took up residence at the university from c. 1656 until 1668. In Oxford he was exposed to the latest developments in natural philosophy and became associated with a group of notable natural philosophers and physicians, including

John Wilkins, Christopher Wren, and John Locke. These individuals, together with a few others, formed the "Experimental Philosophy Club," which at times convened in Boyle's lodgings. Much of Boyle's best-known work dates from this period.

In 1659 Boyle and Robert Hooke, the clever inventor and subsequent curator of experiments for the Royal Society, completed the construction of their famous air pump and used it to study pneumatics. Their resultant discoveries regarding air pressure and the vacuum appeared in Boyle's first scientific publication, *New Experiments Physico-Mechanicall, Touching the Spring of the Air and its Effects* (1660). Boyle and Hooke discovered several physical characteristics of air, including its role in combustion, respiration, and the transmission of sound. One of their findings, published in 1662, later became known as "Boyle's law." This law expresses the inverse relationship that exists between the pressure and volume of a gas, and it was determined by measuring the volume occupied by a constant quantity of air when compressed by differing weights of mercury. Other natural philosophers, including Henry Power and Richard Towneley, concurrently reported similar findings about air.

Boyle's scientific work is characterized by its reliance on experiment and observation and its reluctance to formulate generalized theories. He advocated a "mechanical philosophy" that saw the universe as a huge machine or clock in which all natural phenomena were accountable purely by mechanical, clockwork motion. His contributions to chemistry were based on a mechanical "corpuscularian hypothesis"—a brand of atomism which claimed that everything was composed of minute (but not indivisible) particles of a single universal matter and that these particles were only differentiable by their shape and motion. Among his most influential writings were *The Sceptical Chymist* (1661), which assailed the then-current Aristotelian and especially

Paracelsian notions about the composition of matter and methods of chemical analysis, and the *Origine of Formes and Qualities* (1666), which used chemical phenomena to support the corpuscularian hypothesis.

Boyle also maintained a lifelong pursuit of transmutational alchemy, endeavoring to discover the secret of transmuting base metals into gold and to contact individuals believed to possess alchemical secrets. Overall, Boyle argued so strongly for the need of applying the principles and methods of chemistry to the study of the natural world and to medicine that he later gained the appellation of the "father of chemistry."

ANTONIE VAN LEEUWENHOEK
(b. Oct. 24, 1632, Delft, Neth.—d. Aug. 26, 1723, Delft)

Dutch microscopist Antonie van Leeuwenhoek was the first to observe bacteria and protozoa. His researches on lower animals refuted the doctrine of spontaneous generation, and his observations helped lay the foundations for the sciences of bacteriology and protozoology. The dramatic nature of his discoveries made him world famous, and he was visited by many notables—including Peter I of Russia, James II of England, and Frederick II of Prussia.

Little is known of Leeuwenhoek's early life. When his stepfather died in 1648, he was sent to Amsterdam to become an apprentice to a linendraper. Returning to Delft when he was 20, he established himself as a draper and haberdasher. In 1660 he obtained a position as chamberlain to the sheriffs of Delft. His income was thus secure and sufficient enough to enable him to devote much of his time to his all-absorbing hobby, that of grinding lenses and using them to study tiny objects.

Leeuwenhoek made microscopes consisting of a

single, high-quality lens of very short focal length; at the time, such simple microscopes were preferable to the compound microscope, which increased the problem of chromatic aberration. Although Leeuwenhoek's studies lacked the organization of formal scientific research, his powers of careful observation enabled him to make discoveries of fundamental importance. In 1674 he began to observe bacteria and protozoa, his "very little animalcules," which he was able to isolate from different sources, such as rainwater, pond and well water, and the human mouth and intestine, and he calculated their sizes.

In 1677 he described for the first time the spermatozoa from insects, dogs, and man, though Stephen Hamm probably was a codiscoverer. Leeuwenhoek studied the structure of the optic lens, striations in muscles, the mouthparts of insects, and the fine structure of plants, and discovered parthenogenesis in aphids. In 1680 he noticed that yeasts consist of minute globular particles. He extended Marcello Malpighi's demonstration in 1660 of the blood capillaries by giving (in 1684) the first accurate description of red blood cells. In his observations on rotifers in 1702, Leeuwenhoek remarked that "in all falling rain, carried from gutters into water-butts, animalcules are to be found; and that in all kinds of water, standing in the open air, animalcules can turn up. For these animalcules can be carried over by the wind, along with the bits of dust floating in the air."

A friend of Leeuwenhoek put him in touch with the Royal Society, to which, from 1673 until 1723, he communicated by means of informal letters most of his discoveries and to which he was elected a fellow in 1680. His discoveries were for the most part made public in the society's *Philosophical Transactions*. The first representation of bacteria is to be found in a drawing by Leeuwenhoek in that publication in 1683.

His researches on the life histories of various low forms of animal life were in opposition to the doctrine that they could be produced spontaneously or bred from corruption. Thus, he showed that the weevils of granaries (in his time commonly supposed to be bred from wheat as well as in it) are really grubs hatched from eggs deposited by winged insects. His letter on the flea, in which he not only described its structure but traced out the whole history of its metamorphosis, is of great interest, not so much for the exactness of his observations as for an illustration of his opposition to the spontaneous generation of many lower organisms, such as "this minute and despised creature." Some theorists asserted that the flea was produced from sand, others from dust or the like, but Leeuwenhoek proved that it bred in the regular way of winged insects.

Leeuwenhoek also carefully studied the history of the ant and was the first to show that what had been commonly reputed to be ants' eggs were really their pupae, containing the perfect insect nearly ready for emergence, and that the true eggs were much smaller and gave origin to maggots, or larvae. He argued that the sea mussel and other shellfish were not generated out of sand found at the seashore or mud in the beds of rivers at low water but from spawn, by the regular course of generation. He maintained the same to be true of the freshwater mussel, whose embryos he examined so carefully that he was able to observe how they were consumed by "animalcules," many of which, according to his description, must have included ciliates in conjugation, flagellates, and the *Vorticella*. Similarly, he investigated the generation of eels, which were at that time supposed to be produced from dew without the ordinary process of generation.

Leeuwenhoek's methods of microscopy, which he kept secret, remain something of a mystery. During his lifetime he ground more than 400 lenses, most of which were very small—some no larger than a pinhead—and usually mounted them between two thin brass plates, riveted together. A large sample of these lenses, bequeathed to the Royal Society, were found to have magnifying powers of between 50 and, at the most, 300 times. In order to observe phenomena as small as bacteria, Leeuwenhoek must have employed some form of oblique illumination, or other technique, for enhancing the effectiveness of the lens, but this method he would not reveal. Leeuwenhoek continued his work almost to the end of his long life of 90 years.

Leeuwenhoek's contributions to the *Philosophical Transactions* amounted to 375 and those to the *Memoirs of the Paris Academy of Sciences* to 27. Two collections of his works appeared during his life, one in Dutch (1685–1718) and the other in Latin (1715–22); a selection was translated by S. Hoole, *The Select Works of A. van Leeuwenhoek* (1798–1807).

ROBERT HOOKE

(b. July 18, 1635, Freshwater, Isle of Wight, Eng.—d. March 3, 1703, London)

English physicist Robert Hooke discovered the law of elasticity, known as Hooke's law. He also conducted research in a remarkable variety of fields.

In 1655 Hooke was employed by Robert Boyle to construct the Boylean air pump. Five years later, Hooke discovered his law of elasticity, which states that the stretching of a solid body (e.g., metal, wood) is proportional to the force applied to it. The law laid the basis for studies of stress and strain and for understanding of elastic materials. He applied these studies in his designs for the balance springs of watches. In 1662 he was appointed curator of experiments to the Royal Society of London and was elected a fellow the following year.

One of the first men to build a Gregorian reflecting telescope, Hooke discovered the fifth star in the Trapezium, an asterism in the constellation Orion, in 1664 and first suggested that Jupiter rotates on its axis. His detailed sketches of Mars were used in the 19th century to determine that planet's rate of rotation. In 1665 he was appointed professor of geometry in Gresham College. In *Micrographia* (1665; "Small Drawings") he included his studies and illustrations of the crystal structure of snowflakes, discussed the possibility of manufacturing artificial fibers by a process similar to the spinning of the silkworm, and first used the word cell to name the microscopic honeycomb cavities in cork. His studies of microscopic fossils led him to become one of the first proponents of a theory of evolution.

Hooke suggested that the force of gravity could be measured by utilizing the motion of a pendulum (1666) and attempted to show that Earth and the moon follow an elliptical path around the sun. In 1672 he discovered the phenomenon of diffraction (the bending of light rays around corners); to explain it, he offered the wave theory of light. He stated the inverse square law to describe planetary motions in 1678, a law that Newton later used in modified form. Hooke complained that he was not given sufficient credit for the law and became involved in bitter controversy with Newton. Hooke was the first man to state in general that all matter expands when heated and that air is made up of particles separated from each other by relatively large distances.

JOHN RAY

(b. Nov. 29, 1627, Black Notley, Essex, Eng.—d. Jan. 17, 1705, Black Notley)

John Ray (spelled Wray until 1670) was a leading 17th-century English naturalist and botanist who contributed significantly to progress in taxonomy. His enduring legacy to botany was the establishment of species as the ultimate unit of taxonomy.

EDUCATION AND EXPEDITIONS

Ray was the son of the village blacksmith in Black Notley and attended the grammar school in nearby Braintree. In 1644, with the aid of a fund that had been left in trust to support needy scholars at the University of Cambridge, he enrolled at one of the colleges there, St. Catherine's Hall, and moved to Trinity College in 1646. Ray had come to Cambridge at the right time for one with his talents, for he found a circle of friends with whom he pursued anatomical and chemical studies. He also progressed well in the curriculum, taking his bachelor's degree in 1648 and being elected to a fellowship at Trinity the following year; during the next 13 years he lived quietly in his collegiate cloister.

Ray's string of fortunate circumstances ended with the Restoration. Although he was never an excited partisan, he was thoroughly Puritan in spirit and refused to take the oath that was prescribed by the Act of Uniformity. In 1662 he lost his fellowship. Prosperous friends supported him during the subsequent 43 years while he pursued his career as a naturalist, which began with the publication of his first work in 1660, a catalog of plants growing around Cambridge. After he had exhausted the Cambridge area as a subject for his studies, Ray began to explore the rest of Britain. An expedition in 1662 to Wales and Cornwall with the naturalist Francis Willughby was a turning point in his life. Willughby and Ray agreed to undertake a study of the complete natural history of living things, with Ray responsible for the plant kingdom and Willughby the animal.

The first fruit of the agreement, a tour of the European continent lasting from 1663 to 1666, greatly extended Ray's firsthand knowledge of flora and fauna. Back in England, the two friends set to work on their appointed task. In 1670 Ray produced a *Catalogus Plantarum Angliae* ("Catalog of English Plants"). Then in 1672 Willughby suddenly died, and Ray took up the completion of Willughby's portion of their project. In 1676 Ray published *F. Willughbeii . . . Ornithologia* (*The Ornithology of F. Willughby . . .*) under Willughby's name, even though Ray had contributed at least as much as Willughby. Ray also completed *F. Willughbeii . . . de Historia Piscium* (1685; "History of Fish"), with the Royal Society, of which Ray was a fellow, financing its publication.

IMPORTANT PUBLICATIONS

Ray had never interrupted his research in botany. In 1682 he had published a *Methodus Plantarum Nova* (revised in 1703 as the *Methodus Plantarum Emendata . . .*), his contribution to classification, which insisted on the taxonomic importance of the distinction between monocotyledons and dicotyledons, plants whose seeds germinate with one leaf and those with two, respectively. Ray's enduring legacy to botany was the establishment of species as the ultimate unit of taxonomy. On the basis of the *Methodus*, he constructed his masterwork, the *Historia Plantarum*, three huge volumes that appeared between 1686 and 1704. After the first two volumes, he was urged to compose a complete system of nature. To this end he compiled brief synopses of British and European plants, a *Synopsis Methodica Avium et Piscium* (published posthumously, 1713; "Synopsis of Birds and Fish"), and a *Synopsis Methodica Animalium Quadrupedum et Serpentini Generis* (1693; "Synopsis of Quadrupeds"). Much of his final decade was spent on a pioneering investigation of insects, published posthumously as *Historia Insectorum*.

In all this work, Ray contributed to the ordering of taxonomy. Instead of a single feature, he attempted to base his systems of classification on all the structural characteristics, including internal anatomy. By insisting on the importance of lungs and cardiac structure, he effectively established the class of mammals, and he divided insects according to the presence or absence of metamorphoses. Although a truly natural system of taxonomy could not be realized before the age of Darwin, Ray's system approached that goal more than the frankly artificial systems of his contemporaries. He was one of the great predecessors who made possible Carolus Linnaeus's contributions in the following century.

Nor was this the sum of his work. In the 1690s Ray also published three volumes on religion. *The Wisdom of God Manifested in the Works of the Creation* (1691), an essay in natural religion that called on the full range of his biological learning, was his most popular and influential book. It argued that the correlation of form and function in organic nature demonstrates the necessity of an omniscient creator. This argument from design, common to most of the leading scientists of the 17th century, implied a static view of nature that was distinctly different from the evolutionary ideas of the early and mid-19th century. Still working on his *Historia Insectorum*, John Ray died at the age of 77.

SIR ISAAC NEWTON

(b. Dec. 25, 1642 [Jan. 4, 1643, New Style], Woolsthorpe, Lincolnshire, Eng.—d. March 20 [March 31], 1727, London)

English physicist and mathematician Sir Isaac Newton was the culminating figure of the scientific revolution of the 17th century. In optics, his discovery of the composition of white light integrated the phenomena of colors into the science of light and laid the foundation for modern physical optics. In mechanics, his three laws of motion, the basic principles of modern physics, resulted in the formulation of the law of universal gravitation. In mathematics, he was the original discoverer of the infinitesimal calculus. Newton's *Philosophiae Naturalis Principia Mathematica* (*Mathematical Principles of Natural Philosophy*), 1687, was one of the most important single works in the history of modern science.

The *Opticks*

Newton was elected to a fellowship in Trinity College in 1667, and from 1670 to 1672 he delivered a series of lectures and developed them into the essay "Of Colours," which was later revised to become Book One of his *Opticks*. Newton held that light consists of material corpuscles in motion. The corpuscular conception of light was always a speculative theory on the periphery of his optics, however. The core of Newton's contribution had to do with colors. He realized that light is not simple and homogeneous—it is instead complex and heterogeneous and the phenomena of colors arise from the analysis of the heterogeneous mixture into its simple components.

The ultimate source of Newton's conviction that light is corpuscular was his recognition that individual rays of light have immutable properties. He held that individual rays (that is, particles of given size) excite sensations of individual colors when they strike the retina of the eye. He also concluded that rays refract at distinct angles—hence, the prismatic spectrum, a beam of heterogeneous rays, i.e., alike incident on one face of a prism, separated or analyzed by the refraction into its component parts—and that phenomena such as the rainbow are produced by refractive analysis. Because he believed that chromatic aberration could never be eliminated from lenses, Newton turned to reflecting telescopes; he constructed the first ever built. The heterogeneity of light has been the foundation of physical optics since his time.

In 1675 Newton brought forth a second paper, an examination of the color phenomena in thin films, which was identical to most of Book Two as it later appeared in the *Opticks*. The purpose of the paper was to explain the colors of solid bodies by showing how light can be analyzed into its components by reflection as well as refraction. The paper was significant in demonstrating for the first time the existence of periodic optical phenomena. He discovered the concentric colored rings in the thin film of air between a lens and a flat sheet of glass; the distance between these concentric rings (Newton's rings) depends on the increasing thickness of the film of air.

A second piece which Newton had sent with the paper of 1675 provoked new controversy. Entitled "An Hypothesis Explaining the Properties of Light," it was in fact a general system of nature. Robert Hooke, who had earlier established himself as an opponent of Newton's ideas, apparently claimed that Newton had stolen its content from him. The issue was quickly controlled, however, by an exchange of formal, excessively polite letters that fail to conceal the complete lack of warmth between the men.

Newton was also engaged in another exchange on his theory of colors with a circle of English Jesuits in Liège, perhaps the most revealing exchange of all. Although their objections were shallow, their contention that his experiments were mistaken lashed him into a fury. The correspondence dragged on until 1678, when a final shriek of rage from Newton, apparently accompanied by a complete nervous breakdown, was followed by silence. For six years he withdrew from intellectual commerce except

The English scientist and mathematician Isaac Newton is seen here creating a shaft of light.

when others initiated a correspondence, which he always broke off as quickly as possible.

During his time of isolation, Newton, who was always somewhat interested in alchemy, now immersed himself in it. His conception of nature underwent a decisive change. Newton's "Hypothesis of Light" of 1675, with its universal ether, was a standard mechanical system of nature. However, about 1679, Newton abandoned the ether and its invisible mechanisms and began to ascribe the puzzling phenomena—chemical affinities, the generation of heat in chemical reactions, surface tension in fluids, capillary action, the cohesion of bodies, and the like—to attractions and repulsions between particles of matter.

More than 35 years later, in the second English edition of the *Opticks*, Newton accepted an ether again, although it was an ether that embodied the concept of action at a distance by positing a repulsion between its particles. As he conceived of them, attractions were quantitatively defined, and they offered a bridge to unite the two basic themes of 17th-century science—the mechanical tradition, which had dealt primarily with verbal mechanical imagery, and the Pythagorean tradition, which insisted on the mathematical nature of reality. Newton's reconciliation through the concept of force was his ultimate contribution to science.

THE *PRINCIPIA*

In 1684 Newton was at work on the problem of orbital dynamics, and two and a half years later, a short tract he had written, entitled *De Motu* ("On Motion"), had grown into *Philosophiae Naturalis Principia Mathematica*. This work is not only Newton's masterpiece but also the fundamental work for the whole of modern science. Significantly, *De Motu* did not state the law of universal gravitation. For that matter, even though it was a treatise on planetary dynamics, it did not contain any of the three Newtonian laws of motion. Only when revising *De Motu* did Newton embrace the principle of inertia (the first law) and arrive at the second law of motion.

The mechanics of the *Principia* was an exact quantitative description of the motions of visible bodies. It rested on Newton's three laws of motion: (1) that a body remains in its state of rest unless it is compelled to change that state by a force impressed on it; (2) that the change of motion (the change of velocity times the mass of the body) is proportional to the force impressed; (3) that to every action there is an equal and opposite reaction. Using these laws, Newton found that the centripetal force holding the planets in their given orbits about the sun must decrease with the square of the planets' distances from the sun.

Newton also compared the distance by which the moon, in its orbit of known size, is diverted from a tangential path in one second with the distance that a body at the surface of the earth falls from rest in one second. When the latter distance proved to be 3,600 (60×60) times as great as the former, he concluded that one and the same force, governed by a single quantitative law, is operative in all three cases, and from the correlation of the moon's orbit with the measured acceleration of gravity on the surface of the earth, he applied the ancient Latin word *gravitas* (literally, "heaviness" or "weight") to it. The law of universal gravitation, which he also confirmed from such further phenomena as the tides and the orbits of comets, states that every particle of matter in the universe attracts every other particle with a force that is proportional to the product of their masses and inversely proportional to the square of the distance between their centers. The *Principia* immediately raised Newton to international prominence.

CAROLUS LINNAEUS

(b. May 23, 1707, Råshult, Småland, Swed.—d. Jan. 10, 1778, Uppsala)

S wedish naturalist and explorer Carolus Linnaeus was the first to frame principles for defining natural genera and species of organisms and to create a uniform system for naming them (binomial nomenclature).

THE "SEXUAL SYSTEM" OF CLASSIFICATION

In 1735 Linnaeus published *Systema Naturae* ("The System of Nature"), a folio volume of only 11 pages, which presented a hierarchical classification, or taxonomy, of the three kingdoms of nature: stones, plants, and animals. Each kingdom was subdivided into classes, orders, genera, species, and varieties. This hierarchy of taxonomic ranks replaced traditional systems of biological classification that were based on mutually exclusive divisions, or dichotomies.

In particular, it was the botanical section of *Systema Naturae* that built Linnaeus's scientific reputation. After reading essays on sexual reproduction in plants by Sébastian Vaillant and by Rudolph Jacob Camerarius, Linnaeus had become convinced of the idea that all organisms reproduce sexually. As a result, he expected each plant to possess male and female sexual organs (stamens and pistils), or "husbands and wives," as he also put it. On this basis, he designed a simple system of distinctive characteristics to classify each plant. The number and position of the stamens, or husbands, determined the class to which it belonged, whereas the number and position of pistils, or wives, determined the order. This "sexual system," as Linnaeus called it, became extremely popular.

Classification by "Natural Characters"

In 1736 Linnaeus, then in the Netherlands, published a booklet, the *Fundamenta Botanica* ("The Foundations of Botany"), that framed the principles and rules to be followed in the classification and naming of plants. The year before, Linnaeus was introduced to George Clifford, a local English merchant and banker who had close connections to the Dutch East India Company. Impressed by Linnaeus's knowledge, Clifford offered Linnaeus a position as curator of his botanical garden. Linnaeus accepted the position and used this opportunity to expand certain chapters of the *Fundamenta Botanica* in separate publications: the *Bibliotheca Botanica* (1736; "The Library of Botany"); *Critica Botanica* (1737; "A Critique of Botany"), on botanical nomenclature; and *Classes Plantarum* (1738; "Classes of Plants"). He applied the theoretical framework laid down in these books in two further publications: *Hortus Cliffortianus* (1737), a catalog of the species contained in Clifford's collection; and the *Genera Plantarum* (1737; "Genera of Plants"), which modified and updated definitions of plant genera first offered by Joseph Pitton de Tournefort.

Genera Plantarum was considered by Linnaeus to be his crowning taxonomic achievement. In contrast to earlier attempts by other botanists at generic definition, which proceeded by a set of arbitrary divisions, *Genera Plantarum* presented a system based on what Linnaeus called the "natural characters" of genera—morphological descriptions of all the parts of flower and fruit. In contrast to systems based on arbitrary divisions (including his own sexual system), a system based on natural characters could accommodate the growing number of new species—often possessing different morphological features—pouring into Europe from its oversea trading posts and colonies.

Linnaeus's distinction between artificial and natural classifications of organisms, however, raised the question of the mechanism that allowed organisms to fall into natural hierarchies. He could only answer this question with regard to species: species, according to Linnaeus, were similar in form because they derived from the same parental pair created by God at the beginning of the world. Linnaeus tried to explain the existence of natural genera, orders, or classes within the context of hybridization; however, the question of natural hierarchies would not receive a satisfying answer until English naturalist Charles Darwin explained similarity by common descent in his *Origin of Species* (1859).

BINOMIAL NOMENCLATURE

In 1738 Linnaeus began a medical practice in Stockholm, Sweden, which he maintained until 1742, when he received the chair in medicine and botany at Uppsala University. Linnaeus built his further career upon the foundations he laid in the Netherlands. Linnaeus used the international contacts to create a network of correspondents that provided him with seeds and specimens from all over the world. He then incorporated this material into the botanical garden at Uppsala, and these acquisitions helped him develop and refine the empirical basis for revised and enlarged editions of his major taxonomic works. During his lifetime he completed 12 editions of the *Systema Naturae*, six editions of the *Genera Plantarum*, two editions of the *Species Plantarum* ("Species of Plants," which succeeded the *Hortus Cliffortianus* in 1753), and a revised edition of the *Fundamenta Botanica* (which was later renamed the *Philosophia Botanica* [1751; "Philosophy of Botany"]).

Linnaeus's most lasting achievement was the creation

of binomial nomenclature, the system of formally classifying and naming organisms according to their genus and species. In contrast to earlier names that were made up of diagnostic phrases, binomial names (or "trivial" names as Linnaeus himself called them) conferred no prejudicial information about the plant species named. Rather, they served as labels by which a species could be universally addressed. This naming system was also implicitly hierarchical, as each species is classified within a genus. The first use of binomial nomenclature by Linnaeus occurred within the context of a small project in which students were asked to identify the plants consumed by different kinds of cattle. In this project, binomial names served as a type of shorthand for field observations. Despite the advantages of this naming system, binomial names were used consistently in print by Linnaeus only after the publication of the *Species Plantarum* (1753).

The rules of nomenclature that Linnaeus put forward in his *Philosophia Botanica* rested on a recognition of the "law of priority," the rule stating that the first properly published name of a species or genus takes precedence over all other proposed names. These rules became firmly established in the field of natural history and also formed the backbone of international codes of nomenclature— such as the Strickland Code (1842)—created for the fields of botany and zoology in the mid-19th century. The first edition of the *Species Plantarum* (1753) and the 10th edition of the *Systema Naturae* (1758) are the agreed starting points for botanical and zoological nomenclature, respectively.

OTHER CONTRIBUTIONS

Toward the end of his life, Linnaeus became interested in other aspects of the life sciences. Of greatest influence were his physico-theological writings, *Oeconomia Naturae*

(1749; "The Economy of Nature") and *Politiae Naturae* (1760; "The Politics of Nature"). Both works were of great importance to Charles Darwin. His studies of plant hybridization influenced the experimental tradition that led directly to the pea plant experiments of Austrian botanist Gregor Mendel.

HENRY CAVENDISH

(b. Oct. 10, 1731, Nice, France—d. Feb. 24, 1810, London, Eng.)

Henry Cavendish was a natural philosopher and is considered to be the greatest experimental and theoretical English chemist and physicist of his age. Cavendish was distinguished for great accuracy and precision in researches into the composition of atmospheric air, the properties of different gases, the synthesis of water, the law governing electrical attraction and repulsion, a mechanical theory of heat, and calculations of the density (and hence the weight) of Earth. His experiment to weigh Earth has come to be known as the Cavendish experiment.

RESEARCH IN CHEMISTRY

Cavendish was a shy man who was uncomfortable in society and avoided it when he could. About the time of his father's death, Cavendish began to work closely with Charles Blagden, an association that helped Blagden enter fully into London's scientific society. In return, Blagden helped to keep the world at a distance from Cavendish. Cavendish published no books and few papers, but he achieved much. Several areas of research, including mechanics, optics, and magnetism, feature extensively in his manuscripts, but they scarcely feature in his published work.

His first publication (1766) was a combination of three short chemistry papers on "factitious airs," or gases produced in the laboratory. He produced "inflammable air" (hydrogen) by dissolving metals in acids and "fixed air" (carbon dioxide) by dissolving alkalis in acids, and he collected these and other gases in bottles inverted over water or mercury. He then measured their solubility in water and their specific gravity and noted their combustibility. Cavendish was awarded the Royal Society's Copley Medal for this paper. Gas chemistry was of increasing importance in the latter half of the 18th century and became crucial for Frenchman Antoine-Laurent Lavoisier's reform of chemistry, generally known as the chemical revolution.

In 1783 Cavendish published a paper on eudiometry (the measurement of the goodness of gases for breathing). He described a new eudiometer of his own invention, with which he achieved the best results to date, using what in other hands had been the inexact method of measuring gases by weighing them. He next published a paper on the production of water by burning inflammable air (that is, hydrogen) in dephlogisticated air (now known to be oxygen), the latter a constituent of atmospheric air. Cavendish concluded that dephlogisticated air was dephlogisticated water and that hydrogen was either pure phlogiston or phlogisticated water. He reported these findings to Joseph Priestley, an English clergyman and scientist, no later than March 1783, but did not publish them until the following year.

The Scottish inventor James Watt published a paper on the composition of water in 1783; Cavendish had performed the experiments first but published second. Controversy about priority ensued. In 1785 Cavendish carried out an investigation of the composition of common (i.e., atmospheric) air, obtaining, as usual, impressively accurate results. He observed that, when he had determined the

amounts of phlogisticated air (nitrogen) and dephlogisticated air (oxygen), there remained a volume of gas
amounting to 1/120 of the original volume of common air.

In the 1890s, two British physicists, William Ramsay
and Lord Rayleigh, realized that their newly discovered
inert gas, argon, was responsible for Cavendish's problem-
atic residue; he had not made an error. What he had done
was perform rigorous quantitative experiments, using
standardized instruments and methods, aimed at repro-
ducible results; taken the mean of the result of several
experiments; and identified and allowed for sources of
error.

Cavendish, as noted before, used the language of the
old phlogiston theory in chemistry. In 1787 he became one
of the earliest outside France to convert to the new anti-
phlogistic theory of Lavoisier, though he remained
skeptical about the nomenclature of the new theory. He
also objected to Lavoisier's identification of heat as having
a material or elementary basis. Working within the framework of Newtonian mechanism, Cavendish had tackled
the problem of the nature of heat in the 1760s, explaining
heat as the result of the motion of matter. In 1783 he published a paper on the temperature at which mercury
freezes and in that paper made use of the idea of latent
heat, although he did not use the term because he believed
that it implied acceptance of a material theory of heat. He
made his objections explicit in his 1784 paper on air. He
went on to develop a general theory of heat, and the man-
uscript of that theory has been persuasively dated to the
late 1780s. His theory was at once mathematical and
mechanical; it contained the principle of the conservation
of heat (later understood as an instance of conservation of
energy) and even contained the concept (although not the
label) of the mechanical equivalent of heat.

EXPERIMENTS WITH ELECTRICITY

Cavendish also worked out a comprehensive theory of electricity. Like his theory of heat, this theory was mathematical in form and was based on precise quantitative experiments. In 1771 he published an early version of his theory, based on an expansive electrical fluid that exerted pressure. He demonstrated that if the intensity of electric force was inversely proportional to distance, then the electric fluid in excess of that needed for electrical neutrality would lie on the outer surface of an electrified sphere; and he confirmed this experimentally. Cavendish continued to work on electricity after this initial paper, but he published no more on the subject.

Beginning in the mid-1780s Cavendish carried out most of his experiments at his house in London. The most famous of those experiments, published in 1798, was to determine the density of Earth. His apparatus for weighing the world was a modification of the Englishman John Michell's torsion balance. The balance had two small lead balls suspended from the arm of a torsion balance and two much larger stationary lead balls. Cavendish calculated the attraction between the balls from the period of oscillation of the torsion balance, and then he used this value to calculate the density of Earth. What was extraordinary about Cavendish's experiment was its elimination of every source of error and every factor that could disturb the experiment and its precision in measuring an astonishingly small attraction, a mere 1/50,000,000 of the weight of the lead balls. The result that Cavendish obtained for the density of Earth is within 1 percent of the currently accepted figure.

The combination of painstaking care, precise experimentation, thoughtfully modified apparatus, and fundamental theory carries Cavendish's unmistakable signature. It is fitting that the University of Cambridge's great physics laboratory is named the Cavendish Laboratory.

JOSEPH PRIESTLEY

(b. March 13, 1733, Birstall Fieldhead, near Leeds, Yorkshire [now West Yorkshire], Eng. — d. Feb. 6, 1804, Northumberland, Pa., U.S.)

English clergyman, political theorist, and physical scientist Joseph Priestley contributed to advances in liberal political and religious thought and in experimental chemistry. He is best remembered for his contribution to the chemistry of gases.

WORK IN ELECTRICITY

In 1765 Priestley met the American scientist and statesman Benjamin Franklin, who encouraged him to publish *The History and Present State of Electricity, with Original Experiments* (1767). In this work, Priestley used history to show that scientific progress depended more on the accumulation of "new facts" that anyone could discover than on the theoretical insights of a few men of genius. This view shaped Priestley's electrical experiments, in which he anticipated the inverse square law of electrical attraction, discovered that charcoal conducts electricity, and noted the relationship between electricity and chemical change.

THE CHEMISTRY OF GASES

In 1767 Priestley began intensive experimental investigations into chemistry. Between 1772 and 1790, he published six volumes of *Experiments and Observations on Different Kinds of Air* and more than a dozen articles in the Royal Society's *Philosophical Transactions* describing his experiments on gases, or "airs," as they were then called. British pneumatic chemists had previously identified three types of gases: air, carbon dioxide (fixed air), and hydrogen (inflammable air). Priestley incorporated an explanation of the chemistry of these gases into the phlogiston theory, according to which combustible substances released phlogiston (an immaterial "principle of inflammability") during burning.

Priestley discovered 10 new gases: nitric oxide (nitrous air), nitrogen dioxide (red nitrous vapor), nitrous oxide (inflammable nitrous air, later called "laughing gas"), hydrogen chloride (marine acid air), ammonia (alkaline air), sulfur dioxide (vitriolic acid air), silicon tetrafluoride (fluor acid air), nitrogen (phlogisticated air), oxygen (dephlogisticated air, independently codiscovered by Carl Wilhelm Scheele), and a gas later identified as carbon monoxide. Priestley's experimental success resulted predominantly from his ability to design ingenious apparatuses and his skill in their manipulation. He gained particular renown for an improved pneumatic trough in which, by collecting gases over mercury instead of in water, he was able to isolate and examine gases that were soluble in water. For his work on gases, Priestley was awarded the Royal Society's prestigious Copley Medal in 1773.

Upon contemplating the processes of vegetation and the "agitation" of seas and lakes, Priestley envisioned the means by which a benevolent nature restored the "common air" that had been "vitiated and diminished" by such "noxious" processes as combustion and respiration. Apart from strengthening his own spiritual views, these observations informed the photosynthesis experiments performed by his contemporaries, the Dutch physician Jan Ingenhousz and the Swiss clergyman and naturalist Jean Senebier.

When confronted by the multitude of diseases that plagued the growing populations in towns and military installations, Priestley designed an apparatus that produced carbonated water, a mixture that he thought would provide medicinal benefit to sufferers of scurvy and various fevers. Although it ultimately proved ineffective in treating these disorders, the "gasogene" that employed this technique later made possible the soda-water industry. Priestley also designed the "eudiometer," which was used in the general movement for sanitary reform and urban design to measure the "purity" (oxygen content) of atmospheric air.

The Discovery of Oxygen and the Chemical Revolution

Priestley's lasting reputation in science is founded upon the discovery he made on Aug. 1, 1774, when he obtained a colorless gas by heating red mercuric oxide. Finding that a candle would burn and that a mouse would thrive in this gas, he called it "dephlogisticated air," based upon the belief that ordinary air became saturated with phlogiston once it could no longer support combustion and life. Priestley was not yet sure, however, that he had discovered a "new species of air." The following October, while in Paris on a journey through Europe, he informed the French chemist Antoine-Laurent Lavoisier how he obtained the new "air." This meeting between the two scientists was highly significant for the future of chemistry. Lavoisier immediately repeated Priestley's experiments and, between 1775 and 1780, conducted intensive investigations from which he derived the elementary nature of oxygen, recognized it as the "active" principle in the atmosphere, interpreted its role in combustion and respiration, and gave it its name. Lavoisier's pronouncements of the activity of oxygen revolutionized chemistry.

In 1800 Priestley published a slim pamphlet, *Doctrine of Phlogiston Established, and That of the Composition of Water Refuted*, which he expanded to book length in 1803. The *Doctrine of Phlogiston* provided a detailed account of what he envisioned to be the empirical, theoretical, and methodological shortcomings of the oxygen theory. Priestley called for a patient, humble, experimental approach to God's infinite creation. Chemistry could support piety and liberty only if it avoided speculative theorizing and encouraged the observation of God's benevolent creation. The phlogiston theory was superseded by Lavoisier's oxidation theory of combustion and respiration.

TURMOIL AND EXILE

The English press and government decreed that Priestley's support, together with that of his friend, the moral philosopher Richard Price, of the American and French Revolutions was "seditious." On July 14, 1791, the "Church-and-King mob" destroyed Priestley's house and laboratory. Priestley and his family retreated to the security of Price's congregation at Hackney, near London. Priestley later began teaching at New College, Oxford, and defended his anti-British government views in *Letters to the Right Honourable Edmund Burke* (1791).

In 1794 Priestley fled to the United States, where he discovered a form of government that was "relatively tolerable." His best-known writing in the United States, *Letters to the Inhabitants of Northumberland* (1799), became part of the Republican response to the Federalists. Priestley died at Northumberland, Pennsylvania, mourned and revered by Thomas Jefferson, the third president of the United States.

LUIGI GALVANI

(b. Sept. 9, 1737, Bologna, Papal States [Italy]—d. Dec. 4, 1798, Bologna, Cisalpine Republic)

Luigi Galvani was an Italian physician and physicist who investigated the nature and effects of what he conceived to be electricity in animal tissue. His discoveries led to the invention of the voltaic pile, a kind of battery that makes possible a constant source of current electricity.

EARLY YEARS

Galvani followed his father's preference for medicine by attending the University of Bologna, graduating in 1759. On obtaining the doctor of medicine degree, with a thesis (1762) *De ossibus* on the formation and development of bones, he was appointed lecturer in anatomy at the University of Bologna and professor of obstetrics at the separate Institute of Arts and Sciences. Beginning with his doctoral thesis, his early research was in comparative anatomy—such as the structure of renal tubules, nasal mucosa, and the middle ear—with a tendency toward physiology, a direction appropriate to the later work for which he is noted.

Galvani's developing interest was indicated by his lectures on the anatomy of the frog in 1773 and in electrophysiology in the late 1770s, when, following the acquisition of an electrostatic machine (a large device for making sparks) and a Leyden jar (a device used to store static electricity), he began to experiment with muscular stimulation by electrical means. His notebooks indicate that, from the early 1780s, animal electricity remained his major field of investigation. Numerous ingenious observations and experiments have been credited to him; in 1786, for example, he obtained muscular contraction in a frog by touching its nerves with a pair of scissors during an electrical storm. He also observed the legs of a skinned frog kick when a scalpel touched a lumbar nerve of the animal while an electrical machine was activated.

Galvani assured himself by further experiments that the twitching was, in fact, related to the electrical action. He also elicited twitching without the aid of the electrostatic machine by pressing a copper hook into a frog's spinal cord and hanging the hook on an iron railing. Although twitching could occur during a lightning storm or with the aid of an electrostatic machine, it also occurred with only a metallic contact between leg muscles and nerves leading to them. A metallic arc connecting the two tissues could therefore be a substitute for the electrostatic machine.

Electrical Nature of Nerve Impulse

Galvani delayed the announcement of his findings until 1791, when he published his essay *De Viribus Electricitatis in Motu Musculari Commentarius (Commentary on the Effect of Electricity on Muscular Motion)*. He concluded that animal tissue contained a heretofore neglected innate, vital force, which he termed "animal electricity," which activated nerve and muscle when spanned by metal probes. He believed that this new force was a form of electricity in addition to the "natural" form that is produced by lightning or by the electric eel and torpedo ray and to the "artificial" form that is produced by friction (i.e., static electricity). He considered the brain to be the most important organ for the secretion of this "electric fluid" and the nerves to be conductors of the fluid to the nerve and muscle, the tissues of which act as did the outer and inner surfaces of the Leyden jar. The flow of this electric fluid provided a stimulus for the irritable muscle fibers, according to his explanation.

Galvani's scientific colleagues generally accepted his views, but Alessandro Volta, the outstanding professor of physics at the University of Pavia, was not convinced by the analogy between the muscle and the Leyden jar.

Deciding that the frog's legs served only as an indicating electroscope, he held that the contact of dissimilar metals was the true source of stimulation; he referred to the electricity so generated as "metallic electricity" and decided that the muscle, by contracting when touched by metal, resembled the action of an electroscope. Furthermore, Volta said that, if two dissimilar metals in contact both touched a muscle, agitation would also occur and increase with the dissimilarity of the metals. Thus Volta rejected the idea of an "animal electric fluid," replying that the frog's legs responded to differences in metal temper, composition, and bulk. Galvani refuted this by obtaining muscular action with two pieces of the same material. Galvani's gentle nature and Volta's high principles precluded any harshness between them. Volta, who coined the term galvanism, said of Galvani's work that "it contains one of the most beautiful and most surprising discoveries."

In retrospect, Galvani and Volta are both seen to have been partly right and partly wrong. Galvani was correct in attributing muscular contractions to an electrical stimulus but wrong in identifying it as an "animal electricity." Volta correctly denied the existence of an "animal electricity" but was wrong in implying that every electrophysiological effect requires two different metals as sources of current. Galvani, shrinking from the controversy over his discovery, continued his work as teacher, obstetrician, and surgeon, treating both wealthy and needy without regard to fee. In 1794 he offered a defense of his position in an anonymous book, *Dell'uso e dell'attività dell'arco conduttore nella contrazione dei muscoli* ("On the Use and Activity of the Conductive Arch in the Contraction of Muscles"), the supplement of which described muscular contraction without the need of any metal. He caused a muscle to contract by touching the exposed muscle of one frog with a nerve of another and thus established for the first time that bioelectric forces exist within living tissue.

Galvani provided the major stimulus for Volta to discover a source of constant current electricity; this was the voltaic pile, or a battery, with its principles of operation combined from chemistry and physics. This discovery led to the subsequent age of electric power. Moreover, Galvani opened the way to new research in the physiology of muscle and nerve and to the entire subject of electrophysiology.

SIR WILLIAM HERSCHEL

(b. Nov. 15, 1738, Hanover, Ger.—d. Aug. 25, 1822, Slough, Buckinghamshire, Eng.)

German-born British astronomer Sir William Herschel was the founder of sidereal astronomy for the systematic observation of the heavens. He discovered the planet Uranus, hypothesized that nebulae are composed of stars, and developed a theory of stellar evolution. He was knighted in 1816.

Discovery of Uranus

The intellectual curiosity that Herschel acquired from his father led him from the practice to the theory of music, which he studied in Robert Smith's *Harmonics*. From this book he turned to Smith's *A Compleat System of Opticks*, which introduced him to the techniques of telescope construction. Herschel soon began to grind his own mirrors. They were ground from metal disks of copper, tin, and antimony in various proportions. He later produced large mirrors of superb quality—his telescopes proved far superior even to those used at the Greenwich Observatory. He also made his own eyepieces, the strongest with a magnifying power of 6,450 times. Herschel's largest instrument, too cumbersome for regular use, had a mirror made of speculum metal, with a diameter of 48 inches (122 cm) and a focal length of 40 feet (12 m). Completed in 1789, it became one of the technical wonders of the 18th century.

In 1781, during his third and most complete survey of the night sky, Herschel came upon an object that he realized was not an ordinary star. It proved to be the planet Uranus, the first planet to be discovered since prehistoric times. Herschel became famous almost overnight. His friend Dr. William Watson Jr. introduced him to the Royal Society of London, which awarded him the Copley Medal for the discovery of Uranus, and elected him a Fellow. He was subsequently appointed as an astronomer to King George III.

Herschel's big telescopes were ideally suited to study the nature of nebulae, which appear as luminous patches in the sky. Some astronomers thought they were nothing more than clusters of innumerable stars the light of which blends to form a milky appearance. Others held that some nebulae were composed of a luminous fluid. However, Herschel found that his most powerful telescope could resolve into stars several nebulae that appeared "milky" to less well equipped observers. He was convinced that other nebulae would eventually be resolved into individual stars with more powerful instruments. This encouraged him to argue in 1784 and 1785 that all nebulae were formed of stars and that there was no need to postulate the existence of a mysterious luminous fluid to explain the observed facts. Nebulae that could not yet be resolved must be very distant systems, he maintained; and, since they seem large to the observer, their true size must indeed be vast—possibly larger even than the star system of which the sun is a member. By this reasoning, Herschel was led to postulate the existence of what later were called "island universes" of stars.

Theory of the Evolution of Stars

In order to interpret the differences between these star clusters, Herschel emphasized their relative densities by contrasting a cluster of tightly packed stars with others in which the stars were widely scattered. These formations showed that attractive forces were at work. In other words, a group of widely scattered stars was at an earlier stage of its development than one whose stars were tightly packed. Thus, Herschel made change in time, or evolution, a fundamental explanatory concept in astronomy.

In 1785 Herschel developed a cosmogony—a theory concerning the origin of the universe: the stars originally were scattered throughout infinite space, in which attractive forces gradually organized them into even more fragmented and tightly packed clusters. Turning then to the system of stars of which the sun is part, he sought to determine its shape on the basis of two assumptions: (1) that with his telescope he could see all the stars in the system, and (2) that within the system the stars are regularly spread out. Both of these assumptions he subsequently had to abandon. But in his studies he gave the first major example of the usefulness of stellar statistics in that he could count the stars and interpret this data in terms of the extent in space of the Galaxy's star system.

Theory of the Structure of Nebulae

On Nov. 13, 1790, Herschel observed a remarkable nebula, which he was forced to interpret as a central star surrounded by a cloud of "luminous fluid." This discovery contradicted his earlier views. Hitherto Herschel had reasoned that many nebulae that he was unable to resolve (separate into distinct stars), even with his best telescopes, might be distant "island universes" (such objects are now known as galaxies). He was able, however, to adapt his earlier theory to this new evidence by concluding that the central star he had observed was condensing out of the surrounding cloud under the forces of gravity. In 1811 he extended his cosmogony backward in time to the stage when stars had not yet begun to form out of the fluid.

In dealing with the structural organization of the heavens, Herschel assumed that all stars were equally bright, so that differences in apparent brightness are an index only of differences in distances. Throughout his career he stubbornly refused to acknowledge the accumulating evidence that contradicted this assumption. Herschel's labors through 20 years of systematic sweeps for nebulae (1783–1802) resulted in three catalogs listing 2,500 nebulae and star clusters that he substituted for the 100 or so milky patches previously known. He also cataloged 848 double stars—pairs of stars that appear close together in space, and measurements of the comparative brightness of stars. He observed that double stars did not occur by chance as a result of random scattering of stars in space but that they actually revolved about each other. His 70 published papers include not only studies of the motion of the solar system through space and the announcement in 1800 of the discovery of infrared rays but also a succession of detailed investigations of the planets and other members of the solar system.

ANTOINE-LAURENT LAVOISIER

(b. Aug. 26, 1743, Paris, France—d. May 8, 1794, Paris)

Antoine-Laurent Lavoisier was a prominent French chemist and leading figure in the 18th-century chemical revolution who developed an experimentally based theory of the chemical reactivity of oxygen and coauthored the modern system for naming chemical substances.

Having also served as a leading financier and public administrator before the French Revolution, he was executed with other financiers during the revolutionary terror.

Pneumatic Chemistry

The chemistry Lavoisier studied as a student was not a subject particularly noted for conceptual clarity or theoretical rigor. Although chemical writings contained considerable information about the substances chemists studied, little agreement existed upon the precise composition of chemical elements or between explanations of changes in composition. Many natural philosophers still viewed the four elements of Greek natural philosophy—earth, air, fire, and water—as the primary substances of all matter. Chemists like Lavoisier focused their attention upon analyzing "mixts" (i.e., compounds), such as the salts formed when acids combine with alkalis. They hoped that by first identifying the properties of simple substances they would then be able to construct theories to explain the properties of compounds.

Pneumatic chemistry was a lively subject at the time Lavoisier became interested in a particular set of problems that involved air: the linked phenomena of combustion, respiration, and what 18th-century chemists called calcination (the change of metals to a powder [calx], such as that obtained by the rusting of iron).

Conservation of Mass

The assertion that mass is conserved in chemical reactions was an assumption of Enlightenment investigators rather than a discovery revealed by their experiments. Lavoisier believed that matter was neither created nor destroyed in chemical reactions, and in his experiments he sought to demonstrate that this belief was not violated. Still he had difficulty proving that his view was universally valid. His insistence that chemists accepted this assumption as a law was part of his larger program for raising chemistry to the investigative standards and causal explanation found in contemporary experimental physics.

While other chemists were also looking for conservation principles capable of explaining chemical reactions, Lavoisier was particularly intent on collecting and weighing all the substances involved in the reactions he studied. His success in the many elaborate experiments he conducted was in large part due to his independent wealth, which enabled him to have expensive apparatus built to his design, and to his ability to recruit and direct talented research associates. Today the conservation of mass is still sometimes taught as "Lavoisier's law," which is indicative of his success in making this principle a foundation of modern chemistry.

PHLOGISTON THEORY

After being elected a junior member of the Academy of Sciences, Lavoisier began searching for a field of research in which he could distinguish himself. Chemists had long recognized that burning, like breathing, required air, and they also knew that iron rusts only upon exposure to air. Noting that burning gives off light and heat, that warm-blooded animals breathe, and that ores are turned into metals in a furnace, they concluded that fire was the key causal element behind these chemical reactions. The Enlightenment German chemist Georg Ernst Stahl provided a well-regarded explanation of these phenomena. Stahl hypothesized that a common "fiery substance" he called phlogiston was released during combustion, respiration, and calcination, and that it was absorbed when these processes were reversed. Although plausible, this theory raised a number of problems for those who wished to explain chemical reactions in terms of substances that could be isolated and measured.

In the early stages of his research Lavoisier regarded the phlogiston theory as a useful hypothesis, but he sought ways either to solidify its firm experimental foundation or to replace it with an experimentally sound theory of combustion. In the end his theory of oxygenation replaced the phlogiston hypothesis, but it took Lavoisier many years and considerable help from others to reach this goal.

Oxygen Theory of Combustion

The oxygen theory of combustion resulted from a demanding and sustained campaign to construct an experimentally grounded chemical theory of combustion, respiration, and calcination. Lavoisier's research in the early 1770s focused upon weight gains and losses in calcination. It was known that when metals slowly changed into powders (calxes), as was observed in the rusting of iron, the calx actually weighed more than the original metal, whereas when the calx was "reduced" to a metal, a loss of weight occurred. The phlogiston theory did not account for these weight changes, for fire itself could not be isolated and weighed. Lavoisier hypothesized that it was probably the fixation and release of air, rather than fire, that caused the observed gains and losses in weight. This idea set the course of his research for the next decade.

Along the way, he encountered related phenomena that had to be explained. Mineral acids, for instance, were made by roasting a mineral such as sulfur in fire and then mixing the resultant calx with water. Lavoisier had initially conjectured that the sulfur combined with air in the fire and that the air was the cause of acidity. However, it was not at all obvious just what kind of air made sulfur acidic. The problem was further complicated by the concurrent discovery of new kinds of airs within the atmosphere. British pneumatic chemists made most of these discoveries, with Joseph Priestley leading the effort.

And it was Priestley, despite his unrelenting adherence to the phlogiston theory, who ultimately helped Lavoisier unravel the mystery of oxygen. Priestley isolated oxygen in August 1774 after recognizing several properties that distinguished it from atmospheric air. In Paris at the same time, Lavoisier and his colleagues were experimenting with a set of reactions identical to those that Priestley was studying, but they failed to notice the novel properties of the air they collected. Priestley visited Paris later that year and at a dinner held in his honor at the Academy of Sciences informed his French colleagues about the properties of this new air. Lavoisier, who was familiar with Priestley's research and held him in high regard, hurried back to his laboratory, repeated the experiment, and found that it produced precisely the kind of air he needed to complete his theory. He called the gas that was produced oxygen, the generator of acids. Isolating oxygen allowed him to explain both the quantitative and qualitative changes that occurred in combustion, respiration, and calcination.

THE CHEMICAL REVOLUTION

In the canonical history of chemistry Lavoisier is celebrated as the leader of the 18th-century chemical revolution and consequently one of the founders of modern chemistry. Lavoisier was fortunate in having made his contributions to the chemical revolution before the disruptions of political revolution. By 1785 his new theory of combustion was gaining support, and the campaign to reconstruct chemistry according to its precepts began. One tactic to enhance the wide acceptance of his new theory was to propose a related method of naming chemical substances.

In 1787 Lavoisier and three prominent colleagues published a new nomenclature of chemistry, and it was soon widely accepted, thanks largely to Lavoisier's eminence and the cultural authority of Paris and the Academy of Sciences. Its fundamentals remain the method of chemical nomenclature in use today. Two years later Lavoisier published a programmatic *Traité élémentaire de chimie* (*Elementary Treatise on Chemistry*) that described the precise methods chemists should employ when investigating, organizing, and explaining their subjects. It was a worthy culmination of a determined and largely successful program to reinvent chemistry as a modern science.

PIERRE-SIMON LAPLACE

(b. March 23, 1749, Beaumount-en-Auge, Normandy, France — d. March 5, 1827, Paris)

Pierre-Simon, marquis de Laplace was a French mathematician, astronomer, and physicist and is best known for his investigations into the stability of the solar system. Laplace successfully accounted for all the observed deviations of the planets from their theoretical orbits by applying Sir Isaac Newton's theory of gravitation to the solar system, and he developed a conceptual view of evolutionary change in the structure of the solar system. He also demonstrated the usefulness of probability for interpreting scientific data.

Laplace was the son of a peasant farmer. Little is known of his early life except that he quickly showed his mathematical ability at the military academy at Beaumont. In 1766 Laplace entered the University of Caen, but he left for

Paris the next year, apparently without taking a degree. He arrived with a letter of recommendation to the mathematician Jean d'Alembert, who helped him secure a professorship at the École Militaire, where he taught from 1769 to 1776.

In 1773 he began his major lifework—applying Newtonian gravitation to the entire solar system—by taking up a particularly troublesome problem: why Jupiter's orbit appeared to be continuously shrinking while Saturn's continually expanded. The mutual gravitational interactions within the solar system were so complex that mathematical solution seemed impossible; indeed, Newton had concluded that divine intervention was periodically required to preserve the system in equilibrium. Laplace announced the invariability of planetary mean motions (average angular velocity). This discovery in 1773, the first and most important step in establishing the stability of the solar system, was the most important advance in physical astronomy since Newton. It won him associate membership in the French Academy of Sciences the same year.

Applying quantitative methods to a comparison of living and nonliving systems, Laplace and the chemist Antoine-Laurent Lavoisier in 1780, with the aid of an ice calorimeter that they had invented, showed respiration to be a form of combustion. Returning to his astronomical investigations with an examination of the entire subject of planetary perturbations—mutual gravitational effects—Laplace in 1786 proved that the eccentricities and inclinations of planetary orbits to each other will always remain small, constant, and self-correcting. The effects of perturbations were therefore conservative and periodic, not cumulative and disruptive.

During 1784–85 Laplace worked on the subject of attraction between spheroids; in this work the potential function of later physics can be recognized for the first time. Laplace explored the problem of the attraction of any spheroid upon a particle situated outside or upon its surface. Through his discovery that the attractive force of a mass upon a particle, regardless of direction, can be obtained directly by differentiating a single function, Laplace laid the mathematical foundation for the scientific study of heat, magnetism, and electricity.

Laplace removed the last apparent anomaly from the theoretical description of the solar system in 1787 with the announcement that lunar acceleration depends on the eccentricity of Earth's orbit. Although the mean motion of the moon around Earth depends mainly on the gravitational attraction between them, it is slightly diminished by the pull of the sun on the moon. This solar action depends, however, on changes in the eccentricity of Earth's orbit resulting from perturbations by the other planets. As a result, the moon's mean motion is accelerated as long as Earth's orbit tends to become more circular; but, when the reverse occurs, this motion is retarded. The inequality is therefore not truly cumulative, Laplace concluded, but is of a period running into millions of years. The last threat of instability thus disappeared from the theoretical description of the solar system.

In 1796 Laplace published *Exposition du système du monde* (*The System of the World*), a semipopular treatment of his work in celestial mechanics and a model of French prose. The book included his "nebular hypothesis"— attributing the origin of the solar system to cooling and contracting of a gaseous nebula—which strongly influenced future thought on planetary origin. His *Traité de mécanique céleste* (*Celestial Mechanics*), appearing in five volumes between 1798 and 1827, summarized the results obtained by his mathematical development and application of the law of gravitation. He offered a complete mechanical interpretation of the solar system by devising methods for calculating the motions of the planets and their satellites and their perturbations, including the resolution of tidal problems. The book made him a celebrity.

In 1814 Laplace published a popular work for the general reader, *Essai philosophique sur les probabilités* (*A Philosophical Essay on Probability*). This work was the introduction to the second edition of his comprehensive and important *Théorie analytique des probabilités* (*Analytic Theory of Probability*), first published in 1812, in which he described many of the tools he invented for mathematically predicting the probabilities that particular events will occur in nature. He applied his theory not only to the ordinary problems of chance but also to the inquiry into the causes of phenomena, vital statistics, and future events, while emphasizing its importance for physics and astronomy. The book is notable also for including a special case of what became known as the central limit theorem. Laplace proved that the distribution of errors in large data samples from astronomical observations can be approximated by a Gaussian or normal distribution.

Probably because he did not hold strong political views and was not a member of the aristocracy, he escaped imprisonment and execution during the French Revolution. Laplace was president of the Board of Longitude, aided in the organization of the metric system, helped found the scientific Society of Arcueil, and was created a marquis. He served for six weeks as minister of the interior under Napoleon, who famously reminisced that Laplace "carried the spirit of the infinitesimal into administration."

EDWARD JENNER

(b. May 17, 1749, Berkeley, Gloucestershire, Eng.—d. Jan. 26, 1823, Berkeley)

English surgeon Edward Jenner is best known as the discoverer of vaccination for smallpox. Jenner lived at a time when the patterns of British medical practice and education were undergoing gradual change. During this time, the division between the trained physicians and the apothecaries or surgeons—who acquired their medical knowledge through apprenticeship rather than through academic work—was becoming less sharp, and hospital work was becoming much more important.

Jenner attended grammar school and at the age of 13 was apprenticed to a nearby surgeon. In the following eight years Jenner acquired a sound knowledge of medical and surgical practice. On completing his apprenticeship at the age of 21, he went to London and became the house pupil of John Hunter, who was on the staff of St. George's Hospital and was one of the most prominent surgeons in London. Even more important, however, he was an anatomist, biologist, and experimentalist of the first rank; not only did he collect biological specimens, but he also concerned himself with problems of physiology and function.

The firm friendship that grew between the two men lasted until Hunter's death in 1793. From no one else could Jenner have received the stimuli that so confirmed his natural bent—a catholic interest in biological phenomena, disciplined powers of observation, sharpening of critical faculties, and a reliance on experimental investigation. From Hunter, Jenner received the characteristic advice, "Why think [i.e., speculate]—why not try the experiment?"

In addition to his training and experience in biology, Jenner made progress in clinical surgery. After studying in London from 1770 to 1773, he returned to country practice in Berkeley and enjoyed substantial success. He was capable, skillful, and popular. In addition to practicing medicine, he joined two medical groups for the promotion of medical knowledge and wrote occasional medical papers. He played the violin in a musical club, wrote light verse, and, as a naturalist, made many observations, particularly on the nesting habits of the cuckoo and on bird migration. He also collected specimens for Hunter; many of Hunter's letters to Jenner have been preserved, but Jenner's letters to Hunter have unfortunately been lost. After one disappointment in love in 1778, Jenner married in 1788.

Smallpox was widespread in the 18th century, and occasional outbreaks of special intensity resulted in a very high death rate. The disease, a leading cause of death at the time, respected no social class, and disfigurement was not uncommon in patients who recovered. The only means of combating smallpox was a primitive form of vaccination called variolation—intentionally infecting a healthy person with the "matter" taken from a patient sick with a mild attack of the disease. The practice, which originated in China and India, was based on two distinct concepts: first, that one attack of smallpox effectively protected against any subsequent attack and, second, that a person deliberately infected with a mild case of the disease would safely acquire such protection. It was, in present-day terminology, an "elective" infection—i.e., one given to a person in good health. Unfortunately, the transmitted disease did not always remain mild, and mortality sometimes occurred. Furthermore, the inoculated person could disseminate the disease to others and thus act as a focus of infection.

Jenner had been impressed by the fact that a person who had suffered an attack of cowpox—a relatively harmless disease that could be contracted from cattle—could not take the smallpox—i.e., could not become infected whether by accidental or intentional exposure to smallpox. Pondering this phenomenon, Jenner concluded that cowpox not only protected against smallpox but could be transmitted from one person to another as a deliberate mechanism of protection.

The story of the great breakthrough is well known. In May 1796 Jenner found a young dairymaid, Sarah Nelmes, who had fresh cowpox lesions on her hand. On May 14, using matter from Sarah's lesions, he inoculated an eight-year-old boy, James Phipps, who had never had smallpox. Phipps became slightly ill over the course of the next 9 days but was well on the 10th. On July 1 Jenner inoculated the boy again, this time with smallpox matter. No disease developed; protection was complete. In 1798 Jenner, having added further cases, published privately a slender book entitled *An Inquiry into the Causes and Effects of the Variolae Vaccinae*. The procedure spread rapidly to America and the rest of Europe and soon was carried around the world.

Despite errors and occasional chicanery, the death rate from smallpox plunged. Jenner received worldwide recognition and many honors, but he made no attempt to enrich himself through his discovery and actually devoted so much time to the cause of vaccination that his private practice and personal affairs suffered severely. Parliament voted him a sum of £10,000 in 1802 and a further sum of £20,000 in 1806. Jenner not only received honors but also aroused opposition and found himself subjected to attacks and calumnies, despite which he continued his activities on behalf of vaccination. His wife, ill with tuberculosis, died in 1815, and Jenner retired from public life.

JOHN DALTON

(b. Sept. 5 or 6, 1766, Eaglesfield, Cumberland, Eng.—d. July 27, 1844, Manchester)

English meteorologist and chemist John Dalton was a pioneer in the development of modern atomic theory.

EARLY SCIENTIFIC CAREER

In 1793 Dalton published a collection of essays, *Meteorological Observations and Essays*, on meteorologic topics based on his own observations together with those of his friends John Gough and Peter Crosthwaite. It created little stir at first but contained original ideas that, together with Dalton's more developed articles, marked the transition of meteorology from a topic of general folklore to a serious scientific pursuit.

Dalton upheld the view, against contemporary opinion, that the atmosphere was a physical mixture of approximately 80 percent nitrogen and 20 percent oxygen rather than being a specific compound of elements. He measured the capacity of the air to absorb water vapor and the variation of its partial pressure with temperature. He defined partial pressure in terms of a physical law whereby every constituent in a mixture of gases exerted the same pressure it would have if it had been the only gas present. One of Dalton's contemporaries, the British scientist John Frederic Daniell, later hailed him as the "father of meteorology."

Soon after the publication of the essays, Dalton wrote a description of the defect he had discovered in his own and his brother's vision. This paper was the first publication on color blindness, which for some time thereafter was known as Daltonism.

Atomic Theory

By far Dalton's most influential work in chemistry was his atomic theory. Attempts to trace precisely how Dalton developed this theory have proved futile; even Dalton's own recollections on the subject are incomplete. He based his theory of partial pressures on the idea that only like atoms in a mixture of gases repel one another, whereas unlike atoms appear to react indifferently toward each other. This conceptualization explained why each gas in a mixture behaved independently. Although this view was later shown to be erroneous, it served a useful purpose in allowing him to abolish the idea, held by many previous atomists from the Greek philosopher Democritus to the 18th-century mathematician and astronomer Ruggero Giuseppe Boscovich, that atoms of all kinds of matter are alike. Dalton claimed that atoms of different elements vary in size and mass, and indeed this claim is the cardinal feature of his atomic theory. He focused upon determining the relative masses of each different kind of atom, a process that could be accomplished, he claimed, only by considering the number of atoms of each element present in different chemical compounds.

Although Dalton had taught chemistry for several years, he had not yet performed actual research in this field. In a memoir read to the Manchester Literary and Philosophical Society on Oct. 21, 1803, he claimed: "An inquiry into the relative weights of the ultimate particles of bodies is a subject, as far as I know, entirely new; I have lately been prosecuting this inquiry with remarkable success." He described his method of measuring the masses of various elements, including hydrogen, oxygen, carbon, and nitrogen, according to the way they combined with fixed masses of each other. If such measurements were to be meaningful, the elements had to combine in fixed proportions. His measurements, crude as they were, allowed him to formulate the Law of Multiple Proportions: When two elements form more than one compound, the masses of one element that combine with a fixed mass of the other are in a ratio of small whole numbers. Thus, taking the elements as A and B, various combinations between them naturally occur according to the mass ratios $A{:}B = x{:}y$ or $x{:}2y$ or $2x{:}y$, and so on. Different compounds were formed by combining atomic building blocks of different masses. As the Swedish chemist Jöns Jacob Berzelius wrote to Dalton: "The law of multiple proportions is a mystery without the atomic theory." And Dalton provided the basis for this theory.

The problem remained, however, that a knowledge of ratios was insufficient to determine the actual number of elemental atoms in each compound. For example, methane was found to contain twice as much hydrogen as ethylene. Following Dalton's rule of "greatest simplicity," namely, that AB is the most likely combination for which he found a meretricious justification in the geometry of close-packed spheres, he assigned methane a combination of one carbon and two hydrogen atoms and ethylene a combination of one carbon and one hydrogen atom. This is now known to be incorrect because the methane molecule is chemically symbolized as CH_4 and the ethylene molecule as C_2H_4. Nevertheless, Dalton's atomic theory triumphed over its weaknesses because his foundational argument was correct. However, overcoming the defects of Dalton's theory was a gradual process, finalized in 1858 only after the Italian chemist Stanislao Cannizzaro pointed out the utility of Amedeo Avogadro's hypothesis in determining molecular masses. Since then, chemists have shown the theory of Daltonian atomism to be a key factor underlying further advances in their field. Organic chemistry in particular progressed rapidly once Dalton's theory gained acceptance. Dalton's atomic theory earned him the sobriquet "father of chemistry."

GEORGES CUVIER

(b. Aug. 23, 1769, Montbéliard, France — d. May 13, 1832, Paris)

French zoologist and statesman Baron Georges Cuvier established the sciences of comparative anatomy and paleontology. From 1784 to 1788 Cuvier attended the Académie Caroline (Karlsschule) in Stuttgart, Germany, where he studied comparative anatomy and learned to dissect. After graduation Cuvier served in 1788–95 as a tutor, during which time he wrote original studies of marine invertebrates, particularly the mollusks. His notes were sent to Étienne Geoffroy Saint-Hilaire, a professor of zoology at the Museum of Natural History in Paris, and at Geoffroy's urging Cuvier joined the staff of the museum. For a time the two scientists collaborated, and in 1795 they jointly published a study of mammalian classification, but their views eventually diverged.

Cuvier remained at the museum and continued his research in comparative anatomy. His first result, in 1797, was *Tableau élémentaire de l'histoire naturelle des animaux* ("Elementary Survey of the Natural History of Animals"), a popular work based on his lectures. In 1800–05, he published his *Leçons d'anatomie comparée* ("Lessons on Comparative Anatomy"). In this work, based also on his lectures at the museum, he put forward his principle of the "correlation of parts," according to which the anatomical structure of every organ is functionally related to all other organs in the body of an animal, and the functional and structural characteristics of organs result from their interaction with their environment. Moreover, according to Cuvier, the functions and habits of an animal determine its anatomical form, in contrast to Geoffroy, who held the reverse theory—that anatomical structure preceded and made necessary a particular mode of life.

Cuvier also argued that the anatomical characteristics distinguishing groups of animals are evidence that species had not changed since the Creation. Each species is so well coordinated, functionally and structurally, that it could not survive significant change. He further maintained that each species was created for its own special purpose and each organ for its special function. In denying evolution, Cuvier disagreed with the views of his colleague Jean-Baptiste Lamarck, who published his theory of evolution in 1809, and eventually also with Geoffroy, who in 1825 published evidence concerning the evolution of crocodiles.

While continuing his zoological work at the museum, Cuvier served as imperial inspector of public instruction and assisted in the establishment of French provincial universities. For these services he was granted the title "chevalier" in 1811. He also wrote the *Rapport historique sur les progrès des sciences naturelles depuis 1789, et sur leur état actuel* ("Historical Report on the Progress of the Sciences"), published in 1810. These publications are lucid expositions of the European science of his time.

Meanwhile, Cuvier also applied his views on the correlation of parts to a systematic study of fossils that he had excavated. He reconstructed complete skeletons of unknown fossil quadrupeds. These constituted astonishing new evidence that whole species of animals had become extinct. Furthermore, he discerned a remarkable sequence in the creatures he exhumed. The deeper, more remote strata contained animal remains—giant salamanders, flying reptiles, and extinct elephants—that were far less similar to animals now living than those found in the more recent strata. He summarized his conclusions, first in 1812 in his *Recherches sur les ossements fossiles de quadrupèdes* ("Researches on the Bones of Fossil Vertebrates"), which included the essay "Discours prélim-inaire" ("Preliminary Discourse"), as well as in the expansion of this essay in book form in 1825, *Discours sur les révolutions de la surface du globe* ("Discourse on the Revolutions of the Globe").

Cuvier's work gave new prestige to the old concept of catastrophism according to which a series of "revolu-tions," or catastrophes—sudden land upheavals and floods—had destroyed entire species of organisms and carved out the present features of the earth. He believed that the area laid waste by these spectacular paroxysms, of which Noah's flood was the most recent and dramatic, was sometimes repopulated by migration of animals from an area that had been spared. Catastrophism remained a major geologic doctrine until it was shown that slow changes over long periods of time could explain the fea-tures of the earth.

In 1817 Cuvier published *Le Règne animal distribué d'après son organisation* ("The Animal Kingdom, Distributed According to Its Organization"), which, with its many subsequent editions, was a significant advance over the systems of classification established by Linnaeus. Cuvier showed that animals possessed so many diverse anatomi-cal traits that they could not be arranged in a single linear system. Instead, he arranged animals into four large groups of animals (vertebrates, mollusks, articulates, and radi-ates), each of which had a special type of anatomical organization. All animals within the same group were clas-sified together, as he believed they were all modifications of one particular anatomical type. Although his classifica-tion is no longer used, Cuvier broke away from the 18th-century idea that all living things were arranged in a continuous series from the simplest up to man.

Cuvier's lifework may be considered as marking a

transition between the 18th-century view of nature and the view that emerged in the last half of the 19th century as a result of the doctrine of evolution. By rejecting the 18th-century method of arranging animals in a continuous series in favor of classifying them in four separate groups, he raised the key question of why animals were anatomically different. Although Cuvier's doctrine of catastrophism did not last, he did set the science of palaeontology on a firm, empirical foundation. He did this by introducing fossils into zoological classification, showing the progressive relation between rock strata and their fossil remains, and by demonstrating, in his comparative anatomy and his reconstructions of fossil skeletons, the importance of functional and anatomical relationships.

GLOSSARY

centripetal force: The force that keeps an object moving toward the center of a curved path and constrained to the path.

concentric: Having a common center.

corpuscle: A minute particle.

electroscope: A device for detecting electric charges.

germinate: To begin to grow.

heterogeneous: Made up of parts that are different.

homogeneous: Made up of parts that are the same.

inertia: The property that means something that isn't moving stays still and something that is moving keeps moving until a force acts on either one.

inoculate: To give a person a weakened form of a disease in order to prevent future infection.

naturalist: Someone who studies and knows a great deal about natural history, especially with regard to zoology or botany.

parthenogenesis: Reproduction without fertilization, usually in plants and invertebrates.

sobriquet: A nickname.

solubility: Having the ability to be dissolved in liquid.

spontaneous generation: The false notion that organisms can spring to life from nonliving matter.

taxonomy: The classification of organisms in an ordered way that highlights natural relationships.

FOR MORE INFORMATION

BOOKS

Coates, Eileen S. *Isaac Newton and the Laws of Motion*. New York: PowerKids Press, 2019.

Goes, Peter. *Timeline: Science and Technology: A Visual History of Our World*. Translated by Bill Nagelkerke. Wellington: Gecko Press, 2020.

Kennon, Caroline. *The Scientific Revolution: How Science and Technology Shaped the World*. New York: Lucent Press, 2019.

Moinard, Marie. *Women Discoverers: Top Women in Science*. New York: NBM Graphic Novels, 2021.

WEBSITES

Famous Scientists
www.famousscientists.org
This website offers biographies of famous scientists from a variety of fields and time periods, including women scientists, such as Caroline Herschel.

The Golub Collection
golubcollection.berkeley.edu/
You can get an idea of the tools used in early microscopy by browsing the Golub Collection's microscope models used in the 17th and 18th centuries.

The Royal Society
royalsociety.org
Explore the Royal Society's website to learn how it has encouraged and published scientific discoveries since 1660 and shaped the course of scientific study.

INDEX